WORLD CELEBRATIONS

TET

KATHRYN WALTON

PowerKiDS press.

Published in 2026 by The Rosen Publishing Group, Inc.
2544 Clinton Street, Buffalo, NY 14224

First Edition

Editor: Greg Roza
Book Design: Rachel Rising

Photo Credits: Cover, Rudimencial/iStock.com; pp. 4, 6, 8, 10, 12, 14, 16, 18, 20 Vjom/Shutterstock.com; pp. 5, 9, 15 Dragon Images/Shutterstock.com; p. 7 CravenA/Shutterstock.com; pp. 11, 13 Thanhliemnguyen/Shutterstock.com; p. 17 sonnguyen4241960/Shutterstock.com; p. 19 Makistock/Shutterstock.com; p. 21 Joseph Sohm/Shutterstock.com.

Some of the images in this book illustrate individuals who are models. The depictions do not imply actual situations or events.

Library of Congress Cataloging-in-Publication Data

Names: Walton, Kathryn, 1993- author
Title: Tet / Kathryn Walton.
Description: [Buffalo] : PowerKids Press, [2026] | Series: World celebrations | Includes bibliographical references and index.
Identifiers: LCCN 2025017060 (print) | LCCN 2025017061 (ebook) | ISBN 9781499452259 library binding | ISBN 9781499452242 paperback | ISBN 9781499452266 ebook
Subjects: LCSH: Vietnamese New Year–Juvenile literature
Classification: LCC GT4905 .W28 2026 (print) | LCC GT4905 (ebook) | DDC 394.2614–dc23/eng/20250417
LC record available at https://lccn.loc.gov/2025017060
LC ebook record available at https://lccn.loc.gov/2025017061

Manufactured in the United States of America

CPSIA Compliance Information: Batch #CSPK26. For Further Information contact Rosen Publishing at 1-800-237-9932.

CONTENTS

Kind and Colorful

Tet is the New Year celebration in the country of Vietnam. It's a holiday in a religion called **Buddhism**. Tet celebrates many things. It celebrates Buddhism, Vietnamese **culture**, family, and the start of spring. Tet is a time to be happy, kind, and colorful!

Vietnam

Vietnam is a country in Southeast Asia. More than 101,300,000 people live there. Buddhism is the second largest religion in Vietnam. However, members of other religions also enjoy celebrating Tet. In fact, Tet is the most popular holiday in Vietnam. People celebrate with colorful and lively parades.

Happy Lunar New Year!

People often call this holiday Tet. But it's full name is Tét Nguyên Đán (TET n-WIN DAN). This means "the celebration of the first morning of the first day of the New Year." People greet each other by saying, "Chúc múng Tét Nguyên Đán!" This means "Happy **Lunar** New Year!"

First Day of Spring

Tet is celebrated on the first day of spring in the Vietnamese culture. Tet doesn't land on the same day every year. That's because the people of Vietnam use a different calendar for some holidays. For the year 2025, Tet occurred on January 29.

2025

Year of the What?

Each year, Tet is named after one of 12 animals: snake, horse, goat, monkey, rooster, dog, pig, rat, buffalo, tiger, cat, and dragon. The year 2025 is the year of the snake! After all the animals are used, they start over at the top of the list.

Honoring Others

Tet is a wonderful day! But the Vietnamese also celebrate in the days before Tet. They celebrate in the days after Tet. This is a time to honor many parts of their lives, including **relatives** who have died. It also includes parents, sisters and brothers, grandparents, friends, neighbors, and pets!

Fun Foods

In northern Vietnam, people eat Bánh Chưng during Tet. It is a square of sticky rice mixed with beans and pork, wrapped in large leaves. In the south, Bánh Tét is more popular. It is also made from sticky rice, but it has a different shape. Bánh Tét can also be sweet!

Just Plain Fun!

Tet is fun! In addition to the family, friends, and fun foods, homes are filled with colorful flowers and fruit trees. The night before Tet, people watch **fireworks**! When relatives visit on Tet, children receive red **envelopes** with "lucky money" in them. It's a fun holiday for everyone!

Tet Around the World

Tet is celebrated in Buddhist and Vietnamese communities around the world. One of the largest Tet celebrations in the United States is in Garden Grove, California. It has been held every year since 1982. Many other towns and cities celebrate Tet too! How do you celebrate Tet?

GLOSSARY

Buddhism: A religion of eastern and central Asia that is based on the teachings of Siddhartha Gautama, or the Buddha.

culture: The beliefs and ways of life of a certain group of people.

envelope: A flat container made of paper, as for a letter to someone.

fireworks: A display of explosions and light high in the air created by the burning of chemicals.

lunar: Having to do with the moon.

relative: Someone in your family.

FOR MORE INFORMATION

BOOKS

Pham, Windy. *The Magic of Tét: A Vietnamese Lunar New Year Bilingual Children's Book*. Independently Published, 2024.

Qui, Yobe. *Our Lunar Year, Celebrating Lunar New Year in Asian Communities*. Independently Published, 2019.

WEBSITES

Tet 2025
huyhoa.net/en/Vietnamese-lunar-new-year
Learn more about Tet and the Vietnamese culture here.

Vietnamese Zodiac
www.vietnamonline.com/culture/vietnamese-zodiac.html
Each of the animals celebrated during Tet has its own meaning. Read about them here.

INDEX